It was book week. The children all went
as characters from books they had read.
Biff and Chip looked exactly the same.
"Can you tell who we are?" asked Biff.

"I know," said Anneena. "You are the
twin detectives in the Tintin books."

"You look good," said Chip, "but who
are you?"

"I am Sherlock Holmes, the famous detective," said Anneena. "No crime is too hard for him to solve."

Biff laughed. "Sorry, Anneena. I've never heard of him."

After school Anneena went to play
with Biff. She had a book about Sherlock
Holmes.

"I love detective stories," Anneena said.
"I want to be a detective one day."

Just then, Mum called Biff. "I'm putting
the washing machine on," she said.

Biff took a pile of clothes down for Mum
to wash. While she was gone, the magic key
glowed.

5

Anneena found herself outside a
grand house.

"Oh no!" she said. "I'm not sure
I want an adventure by myself."

Suddenly a carriage raced up to the
front door. A man jumped out, he had a
coat and hat like Anneena's.

"Who are you?" the man demanded.

"I'm a detective," said Anneena.

"You look far too young. When I sent for an assistant, I expected someone older. Well, come on! We have a crime to solve!"

The man ran into the house. A police officer was standing by the door.

"Ah, Mr Holmes," he said. "Inspector Lees is waiting for you."

"The crime took place in the ballroom,"
said Inspector Lees. "No one has left the
room since the theft took place."

"The theft of what?" said Holmes.

"A diamond necklace," the Inspector said.
Two more police officers stood at the door
of a large ballroom. A crowd of people were
standing inside. A woman was crying.

"Lord and Lady Tuckup are having a party for very rich and famous people," said Inspector Lees. "The Duchess of Almond is here. She *was* wearing her diamond necklace."

"Worth millions, I'm sure," added Holmes.
"At ten o'clock," said Lees, "the lights
went out. They came on again almost
at once and no one could have left the
ballroom. Yet the necklace had been stolen."

"Two of my men were at the door all evening," the Inspector went on. "No one has been allowed to move from the spot since the robbery took place."

"Has everyone been searched?" asked
Holmes.

"Yes, and we have searched every part of
the room," said Lees. "The necklace has not
been found. It is a mystery."

"The person who took the necklace must have been standing near the Duchess," said Holmes.

"The maid was standing next to the Duchess," said Lees. "But it couldn't have been her."

"She was holding a huge tray of empty glasses," said Lees.

"I'm *still* holding it!" said the maid. "May I put it down now please? It has been over an hour."

The maid took the tray to a table outside the ballroom. On the way she dropped a glass. Quickly she picked up the broken bits and threw them in a bin.

"Take everyone to the library, Inspector," said Holmes. "Don't let anyone out of your sight. My assistant and I will look for clues. Then we will question each person again."

Anneena and Holmes looked round the empty ballroom.

"Hmm!" said Holmes. "This beats me. No one could have left the ballroom with the necklace. So where is it now?"

Anneena looked round the other room.
She peered into the bin with the broken glass.
At the bottom was a tennis ball with a split
in it.

"How odd to find that!" she said to herself.

In the library, Holmes questioned the maid.

"It was not me, sir," she said. "I was holding a tray of glasses at the time. And I've been searched."

At that moment Anneena ran in. She was
holding a tray of glasses.

"Stop!" cried Anneena. "The maid is the
thief! Don't let her go."

"She stole the necklace! I know how she did it," Anneena said.

They searched the maid again. The necklace was in her pocket.

"But . . ." gasped the Inspector, "we searched her before. She didn't have the necklace."

"So how *did* she get the necklace out of the room?" asked Holmes.

"In this tennis ball," Anneena said. "She quickly pushed the necklace into the split ball and threw it."

"In the dark, the ball flew over the heads of the police officers. It landed softly in the room behind them. It ended up near the table."

"I see," gasped Holmes. "She dropped
the glass so that she could pick the ball up.
Then she took the necklace out of the ball
and dropped the ball in the bin."

"All the glasses were stuck to the tray except the one that she dropped," said Anneena.

"So she could put the tray down quickly, leaving her hands free to steal the necklace," said Holmes.

The maid began to cry.

"You must have been working with someone who could turn the lights off," Lees said to her. "Who was it?"

"It was the butler," sobbed the maid.

"I did a good job solving this case for you," said Holmes. "I caught the thief."

Anneena looked at Holmes and gasped, but the key began to glow.

"Sorry, Anneena," said Biff, coming back into the room.

"Don't worry," said Anneena. "I've been finding out more about Sherlock Holmes."